NOW

AND

FOREVER

DEVOTIONAL

21 WEEKLY MARRIAGE DEVOTIONS

SHANNON WEATHERS

Introduction

I will betroth you to me forever. I will betroth you to me in righteousness and in justice, in steadfast love and in mercy. Hosea 2:19 Marriage is one of God's greatest gifts to mankind. He honored it so much so that he ordained it, blessed it, ordered it, appointed, anointed, and consecrated it. He fashioned it as a reminder of His great coming; our Lord and Savior Jesus Christ coming back for His Bride. Hallelujah! He wanted us to enjoy this great gift here on earth because He understood the glory that a husband and a wife would bring Him and the glory it brings to families.

With that being said, there is an adversary that hates marriage. His only desire is to destroy relationships one family at a time. During my mid-twenties I endured years of a tumultuous marriage that eventually led to divorce. Not only did we encounter such traumatic experiences but other couples suffered in their relationships as well. Then and only then did I realize that marriages regardless of age, race, and culture were under attack. My ex-husband and I were believers that were raised in Christian homes. His folks prided themselves on being married for 20+ years and although my mom never married my dad, she married my stepfather and was an extraordinary wife and mother. Thus, we ended up in divorce court. How could this be? We said that we loved each other and could not live without the other. We vowed that we would stand by each other through the good and the bad. Yet, I became a single mom. As I left the alter, I was left with unanswered questions, unexplained issues, and undeniable pain and grief. For the first time in my life, I became very angry, bitter, and broken.

With time and prayer I realized where we went wrong. Even though the things that eventually ended our relationship had nothing to do with the choices I made, I realize that I did not have the proper tools to fight while we were going through. I also had some growing up to do. I decided to ask God to heal me from my hurt and prepare me to be a better wife for the husband that He was going to give me. I believed by faith that I was destined to be a wife, a good wife and I refused to let my anger, bitterness, and brokenness keep me from all that God had for me.

Today I believe that I am a healed woman. Not only healed, but I am a blessed, loving, and a whole woman. I pray that you will never experience anything as tragic as a divorce. If you already have, my one hope is that you will receive the healing you need and these short narratives will not only give you a tiny peek into the lives of two imperfect people who are deeply in love with each other but will help guide your actions towards long-lasting love and relationship.

"You come to love not by finding the perfect person, but by seeing an imperfect person perfectly." _Sam Keen

NOW
AND
FOREVER
DEVOTIONAL

Emotionally Intoxicated...

Have you ever met anyone who was inebriated or high on illegal drugs? Typically, they are consumed by their own emotions and actions. Often times they are easy to spot because not only do they distinctly take on physical change with the variation of odd behavior but their actions can result in withdrawal and/or aggression amongst other things. The underlying problem goes beyond what the alcohol or drug does to the abuser, but what the abuser does to the people that love them. Love ones normally experience the blunt of the withdrawal, aggression, and abuse. The drug user or alcoholic however, seems to be oblivious to the negative impact it has caused on their family members and friends; even to themselves.

When we are emotionally sick, we can take on some of the same characteristics of an abuser and our spouse becomes the dumping ground for our emotional junk. During these low periods of our lives, we sometimes expect our spouse to be everything to us when the truth of the matter is; they cannot. It is up to you to settle your emotional disputes. It is your job to help yourself to emotional, mental, and physical healthiness. Yes, your spouse should support you in the process of becoming whole, but you are as equally responsible if not totally in control of your own mental, emotional, and physical state. If you need your spouse to be patient with you while you heal, ask for what you need. But, please remember they are a support system only and not a counselor. They are a pillar for you to lean on and not your legs to stand. Their sole purpose during your healing process is to serve you, encourage you, and pray for you; not to complete the process for you.

Scripture says in *Exodus 7:11, "And it came to pass, when Moses held up his hand, Israel prevailed: and when he let down his hand, Amalek prevailed."* If you read the entire chapter, you will find Moses lifting up his own hands and Israel prevailing, however, after a while he became weary as we all do. When you are fighting a battle to become better it is probable that you will grow tired. *"But don't grow weary in well doing for you will reap if you faint not." Galatians 6:9.* When you are at a point when you feel like all hope is gone; that is a perfect opportunity for God to show Himself mighty in your situation. He will either do it Himself or in Moses' case, He sent him help. *Exodus 7:12-13, "But Moses' hands were heavy; and they took a stone, and put it under him, and he sat thereon; and Aaron and Hur stayed up his hands, the one on the one side, and the other on the other side; and his hands were steady until the going down of the sun."*

It is ok if you grow tired. Healing is a process and it can be a journey that zaps your strength. However, if you have someone in your corner that is willing to hold your arms up, hold your head up, and hold your heart up; my sister and my brother, you will be restored.

Do not fail to decipher the issues that you are struggling with. Realize that those issues are not theirs, but are indeed yours. Now go and apologize to the one you love for putting unnecessary weight on your relationship.

Conversation:

1. I have a confession to make: I am struggling emotionally because...
2. How do I make you feel when I lash out at you?
3. What are some ways that I can effectively communicate what I need from you?

Prayer:

Heavenly Father, in the name of Jesus, forgive me for not taking ownership for my own actions. Past hurt and pain has caused me to lash out on my love ones because I have a hard time effectively communicating my wants and needs. Please take this overwhelming feeling that I have away from me. Sometimes I feel like I have to complete every single task on my to-do list and when it appears that I am far from being finished, I work myself into a frenzy and nothing gets done. The idea of failure enters into my mind and eventually seeps into my heart. My mind takes off like a whirlwind and everything becomes an issue and it's everyone else's fault but my own. I realize I have to accept the things that I cannot change. Please forgive me. I understand the time that has passed, broken relationships, and the issues that I emotionally struggle with will one day all be restored. Help me to forgive myself. Help my spouse to forgive me. Help me set goals and cross them off my list so I can start to enjoy the sense of accomplishment in my life and not defeat. In Jesus name, Amen.

Recommendations:

1. Repent to God and to your spouse (take healing process seriously-2nd chances are not always an option)
2. Seek counseling (even if it is 3 sessions- a little can go a long way)
3. Be willing to tackle one situation at a time.

THE FUMBLE...

Sometimes in your relationship your spouse will do something silly that may try your patience, cost you time, and may even cost you money. These types of situations seem to always present themselves at the most inopportune time. For instance, when the bills are due and you barely have enough to cover them and your spouse gets hit with a speeding ticket. I know what you are thinking; this situation could have been avoided if he/she would have just taken the time to leave a little earlier. Or, what about the times when you missed grand opportunities because your spouse caused you to be late to an appointment, late for an interview, or simply late for the opening of a highly anticipated show that you paid to see. No one situation is greater than the other because it really just boils down to what is important to you. If you feel that your spouse does not care enough to limit what appears to be inconsiderateness; it will take you completely over the edge. When this happens, do not lose your cool with your spouse; your job is to cover them.

I call these hiccups in marriage, The Fumble(s). At my son's football practice, when a teammate or the opposing team drops the ball they are taught to yell "fumble!" At that moment, the players job is to jump on the football and cover it. What I like about this is no one is concerned with why the ball was fumbled or how clumsy the player must have been to lose the football. At that moment all of the players on the offense focus switches to now helping their teammate recover the ball. Keep in mind, all players on the field focus switches to recovery mode. So that means if you do not recover the fumbled ball, a defensive player will. The defense wants the football just as much as you do. When the other team recovers the fumble, if they do not score a touchdown on that play, they will have three more attempts to score points. Sister, do not allow another woman to recover your husband's fumble. My brother, do not allow another man to recover your wife's fumble. In other words, you are not the only one that wants to play on your spouse's team…

In our relationships we have to learn to cover our spouse's fumble. Sure, it cost you money. Okay, it may have made you late. Welp, it's like the third time and it seems as though they will never get it right. Careful! You could begin to develop thoughts towards your spouse that could potentially transform from satisfaction to believing that they are selfish. If you trust your husband or wife really loves you, you have to ask yourself; are they really that unreliable? I think maybe they are just unaware of how they are making you feel when these things happen, whatever "these" things may be. In addition, you may even think that your spouse is the only one to blame, but I would lend to believe that both parties have to own up to the responses of what happens in these types of situations versus weighing so heavily on the incident itself.

When it happens again and believe me it will, take a deep breath and relax. In relationships, progress is your companion and every situation does not require a three round fight. With time, it will get better and until it does; cover your spouse's fumble in love, in peace, and in prayer because when the tables turn, you are going to need them to extend grace and cover yours.

Conversation:

1. I Fumbled. Forgive me.
2. When I mess up, your response makes me feel like...
3. In the future I will work on my areas of weakness but I need you to be patience with me in these areas?

Prayer: Heavenly Father, in the name of Jesus, thank you for another opportunity to get it right. Thank You for shedding light on these areas of darkness in my life. I ask You to make me brave enough to deal with the issues I face daily that causes me to ignore, deny, and disappoint spouse. Make me a better problem solver and a better spouse. In Jesus name, Amen.

You are one...

Do not allow people to treat you like an individual when you are married. You and your spouse are one. In Christ you are one spirit and one flesh. When Christ sees you, He sees both you and your spouse. People who do not value the sanctity of marriage will deliberately fail to acknowledge your spouse and it is disrespectful. If they dishonor your spouse, beloved, they have dishonored you. It is not cute or cool to carry on in this manner when you're married. Check folk or in other words set the record straight on what is and what is not appropriate for you and your spouse. Finally, do not let people subliminally divide you regardless of who they are.

Ex. If your spouse made a decision about "anything" both of you have already made the decision. If someone compliments you on how good of a job you are doing raising your children, make sure you tell them "thank you, WE do our best." If your spouse has spoken to the family about an issue, both of you have already had a discussion with the family. If they have heard from you, essentially they have already heard from the both of you. It's kind of how children try and play one parent off of the other. In my house, if Daddy says no, Mommy's answer is also no. You will find adults who will try and play the same games with you and your spouse. The solution is simple, discern what is happening and deal with it accordingly.

That is why a man leaves his father and mother and is united to his wife, and they become one flesh. (Genesis 2:24)

As long as you allow individuals to treat you like the other doesn't exist, they will. Remember you and your spouse are one. One on the same team. If one loses, you both lose. However, if one wins, you both win.

Conversation:

1. Have we ever allowed anyone to treat us like individuals?
2. Who are they?
3. Why do you think we allow it?
4. What can we do to change it?

Prayer: Heavenly Father, in the name of Jesus, thank You for blessing us with love and relationship. What we have is special because we believe that You have made us especially for each other. We do not want to take our lives together for granted, nor do we want to allow anyone or anything to come before and between the love and union that we share. We ask that You would expose the divider or the thing that comes to divide us. Allow us to be on one accord when we see it or them for what it is or they are. Do not allow us to continue to fall prey to it but be assertive and stop it in its tracks. We believe that we are stronger together and we can put 10,000 to flight. No longer will we live separately in the eyes of others and in the eyes of You. They will know that we are one and will treat us as one. In Jesus name, Amen!

Team _____(write your last name)

Periodically, I think it is smart to "check in" with your spouse. I am suggesting that you simply ask "how are you?" And ask "what can I do to be better for you?"

This is important because if you truly love your spouse you should have a genuine interest in their wellbeing. I have discovered in my adult life that you can be in a relationship with someone, think everything is ok, and never see the pressure building up on the inside of them until the blow up. Spouses please be honest about your feelings. Your spouse cannot help you if they do not know.

What can I do to be better for you?
Having this conversation requires a great deal of patience and maturity. I have met many couples who have become very comfortable and complacent in their relationships to the point they no longer think it is important or they no longer find value in being a better husband or a better wife for their spouse. Rethink this. You owe it to the one you love to consistently evolve, not change; there's a difference. Married couples should grow together whether that be education, promotion, weight loss, or whatever. Choose it and grow in that together.

1. Carve out the time to wrap.
2. Don't nitpick and don't argue.
3. Don't get upset when you learn you have work to do.

Communication makes you better. The goal is to be better.

Conversation:

1. How are you?
2. What can I do to be better for you?
3. What can we do together to be a better team?

Prayer: Heavenly Father, in the name of Jesus, forgive us for letting some things slip. We have treated our relationship like a bill that we have neglected to pay. Not because we didn't have the money but because we just wanted to spend it elsewhere. Because we chose to ignore our needs and not caring for each other the way we should, just like that past due, delinquent, about to shut off notice that we get due to negligence; so is the relationship. We have paid visits to family and friends, spent time working, and invested in projects or extracurricular activities before we did so at home. Today we make a stand that our relationship to each other is more important than any job, any hobby, an extended family member, or any friend. From this point on, we will put the needs of this relationship first. Lord, hold us up through the process and do not let us fall. In Jesus name, Amen.

Can I get a kiss goodnight...

Before bed I always pull the covers back for my hunny. It is my way of welcoming him to bed. The things that happen in our bedroom are sacred; pillow talk, kisses, hugs, and love. Therefore my goal is to always invite him to a place where no one else can go.

Because he loves that small little detail of care I add to his life; if he makes it to bed before I, he pulls the covers back for me as well. Finally, we never let the sun go down without kissing each other good night.

Conversation:

1. Before we go to bed I would like.
2. Let's take this_____ out of our schedule so we can have more time for each other at night.
3. I want to bring this to our bedroom. (Keep it Holy ☺)

Prayer: Heavenly Father, in the name of Jesus, thank You for the bedroom. Thank You for the pleasure of intimacy, love, and love making. Please continue to ignite our fire for each other and do not let it ever burn out. Allow us to see the value in intimacy and help us keep the heat in our romance. Keep our conversations open and fluid and with each passing day take us from glory to glory in our bedroom. In Jesus name, Amen!

Protect your Garden...

In your relationship you will be faced with all kinds of drama, mayhem, and foolishness. Some of which may come from the two of you. However, once you and your spouse have had time to endure some things together; your problem solving skills should become sharper and you should have a better idea of what buttons not to push. You will notice that if you and your spouse are not causing or creating the drama in your life, most of your issues and heartache will come from outside influences. When the enemy fails at his attacks against you and your spouse with your own affairs, he will try and trick you with the mistakes that others make and use those who are closes to you to frazzle you.

It is imperative that you learn the importance of "protecting your garden."

Genesis 2:15 And the Lord God took the man, and put him into the Garden of Eden to dress it and to keep it.

Dress it: When God placed man and woman in the garden He gave them specific instructions. He told them to dress it. That word dress is interpreted as "embellish." God wanted Adam and Eve to make the garden better than it was when He gave it to them. Whatever had to be done to create a better, more comfortable living environment was Adam's and Eve's job. Your job includes some of the same tasks. It is your responsibility to make whatever you have with your spouse better. For example, if you live in a hut, it should be the fanciest hut anyone has ever seen. If you drive a hooptie, keep it clean like a Mercedes Benz AMG. Together you and your spouse should make what you have great and show God that your heart is grateful with whatever and however He blesses you.

Keep it:

The word "keep" means to guard and protect. I can imagine in the garden Adam and Eve were to till the ground, pull the weeds, and upkeep the basic garden needs perhaps. I believe our vocation in marriage is very similar today. "Till the ground" means to plow, prepare, or get ready to plant seed. It is imperative to leave outside influences, outside issues, and anything that does not pertain to your marriage outside. That's not to say you have to turn a blind eye to the things that may be affecting others. You do not have to solve their problems; you can pray for them and love them from a distance. If your relationship is constantly bogged down with the wants and needs of others, you and your spouse will never be able to work on your marriage; plant your goals, plant your dreams, and watch them grow.

Dress it and keep it means to guard and to preserve. If Adam and Eve did not work to dress the Garden, God was warning them that it would deteriorate. That is the way of all things physical; they degenerate if they are not maintained and taken care of. So is your relationship. If not maintained, not dressed, and not kept- it will diminish and deteriorate. Protect your garden.

Conversation:

1. What outside influences have we allowed to enter into our garden?
2. What is the plan to begin to dress and keep our garden?
3. What are some new goals and new dreams we will begin to plant after the ground is ready?

Prayer:

Heavenly Father, in the name of Jesus, thank You for exposing the opposition that has come against our marriage. We have not adequately protected it and have not monitored who we allowed in it. We ask that You forgive us and thank You for another opportunity to make this a place of sacredness. We are aware of who came in invited and uninvited. We are aware of what has been growing illegally in our garden and now we have a plan to uproot anything or anyone that does not benefit our marriage. Thank You for giving us strength to endure when things get tough. We believe that your word will be our muscle to fight off temptation and we believe the Holy Spirit will make us brave enough to handle it. In Jesus name, Amen.

Get it Right or Redo it!

In the beginning stages of our marriage finances were tight like most marriages, but we made it work. I remember once before pay day I took a peek in the fridge and realized that all we had was a half of bag of lettuce, two tough pieces of left over steak, a couple of sweet potatoes in a bag, two cans of tomato soup, shredded cheese, and a few pieces of bread. It may sound pitiful and you maybe be thinking it is downright pathetic, but to me, we had a full course meal. This was really not the time to remind my husband of what we did not have. I am sure he saw what was in the fridge before I did so instead of getting all emotional by yelling, screaming, and getting upset at him because of our lack; I decided to take a different approach.

I took the potatoes, washed them thoroughly, and put them in the oven. While they were baking, I took three bowls, chopped up the lettuce, and divvy up enough salad for husband, my son, and myself. I added a few croutons, bacon bits, and shredded cheese on top. I then opened the cans of tomato soup, poured it in a pot, and added some seasoning with feta cheese to make it creamy. Then I took my steak and seared it enough to bring back the flavor. Finally, I took the two sweet potatoes, opened them up, added butter, sugar, and brown sugar to taste.

By the time my husband and son came down to dinner I had everything prepared. Candles were glowing, the music was flowing, and a big smile was on my face. "Dinner is served my loves." I said. My hunny looked at me in amazement wondering how but did not ask. We just ate, talked, laughed and enjoyed our meal. After dinner we put our son to bed, enjoyed our evening, and before long, my husband was fast asleep.

I sat there with a grateful heart because my family was fed. It really didn't matter what tomorrow was going to bring because if my God fed us today, surely He was big enough to feed us tomorrow. This situation taught me several lessons.

1. Change my perception of the situation.
2. Take the little and make the most of it.
3. Reduce and minimize the amount of stress on my husband and family.
4. Trust God.

I couldn't tell you what we ate the next day. I know we ate something or another because as of yet, we have not missed any meals and we have never been hungry. It is not always what you go through; sometimes your response determines how long you will stay there.

Get it right the first time. Get your attitude right the first time. Get your response right the first time. Get it all the way right so you will be able to move forward to the next big thing.

Conversation:

1. What issue have we constantly had to revisited?
2. What is our attitude during the conflict?
3. How do we respond? Is it positive?

Prayer: Heavenly Father please forgive us for not trusting You in the tough times. We allow our attitudes and emotions to get the best of us and because of our lack of trust in each other, our actions reflect our lack of trust and love for You. We have no desire to be like the children of Israel, a hopeless wonder, wondering for years. We want to get it right this time. Forgive us for our attitude towards our spouse. We have taken a lot of frustration out on each other because we haven't really learned yet how to fully trust You and trust the God in our spouse. Help us to do better. In Jesus name, Amen.

Let's talk about Sex...

It is not unusual for me to pick up a book about anything that I know nothing about and read it. No one has to share with me that it is a good read for me to seek interest. I personally have always been a knowledge connoisseur. My goal is to feel better, look better, and almost always do better. Thus, in a previous relationship I found myself at Barnes & Nobles perusing through the relationship aisle. My hope was to find a book that would in some way help my rapidly declining relationship. I thought there would be mounds of literature consistent with communication, forgiveness, and tools on restoration. At least that is what I was looking for because those were few of the many unfortunates in my relationship. However, from the erotic book selection I had to choose from, it appeared that the whole world was sexually frustrated. Every book was about sex in relationships or the lack thereof. How could this be? Not that I am condoning such behavior, but with all the sex a person can easily indulge in over the internet, TV, and social media; why on earth would there be the need for an entire section on sex, sex, sex? What I soon discovered was 50% of married couples were dissatisfied with their bedroom escapades. While another 37% felt their time between the sheets ended too quickly. That number maybe alarming but it's true. Most individuals who have sex are very dissatisfied, hence the reason for all the books on igniting your sex life. So why is this an issue?

One of the top reasons why marriages end in divorce is because of the unfulfillment of intimacy. When a couple has a declining sex life, the intimacy between the two will also decline. It is imperative that you put just as much time and effort in love making as you do in taking care of your kids. Making love to your spouse should be a top priority. In fact every time you get the opportunity, you and your spouse should be in the bed.... making love. You should despise predictability and fall in love with spontaneity. You should go through extreme measures to keep your relationship fruitful, exhilarating, and divine in the bedroom.

Now that you know, stop talking about sex; be about sex. Making love is the will of God.

Conversation:
1. Are we predictable?
2. Do we make love enough?
3. What would you want more of?

Prayer: Heavenly Father, in the name of Jesus, thank You for giving us a tool to quench our fire. Thank You for giving us a tiny particle of Heaven to enjoy here on earth. I pray that You will keep the fire lit between my spouse and I. May Your name be glorified in our relationship, in our marriage, and in our bedroom. In Jesus name, Amen.

Change Clothes & Go!

For the first two years of my marriage, my mother and father in-law came to live with my husband and I. I wish to God I could tell you that every day was peaches and cream, but I would be lying if I did. It was extremely difficult to live with our parents as adults. Just think about it. There were four, strong willed, and somewhat opinionated individuals living under a two level, 2800 square feet of space that sometimes did not appear to be large enough. However, I would also be lying if I did not tell you that it had extreme benefits because it did.

My in-laws were in home house cleaners, cooks, and baby sitters. It was a sheer blessing to come home after working a 10 hour shift to a clean home and a home cooked meal. Because of the many conveniences they provided and the opportunity for alone time it afforded my husband and I, we took it. We went on vacations around the world, weekend trips, and lots and lots of date nights. The best part about some of our dates was how sporadic they were and I loved it!

Once we moved back east, things changed. Each of us, meaning my husband and I and his folks went our separate ways and the quick get-a-ways were few and far between. Not having a babysitter did not stop us from dating, it simply meant we had to switch things up a bit and be a little more sophisticated with our planning.

I think the best date since the transition was when my husband and I decided that we were not going to wait for a show to come to town to be entertained. We just decided that we would get all dressed up, go to the movies, and have dinner. It was so much fun. We dialogued about current events, work, school, and what we enjoyed most about the movie. It was simply beautiful gazing into my husband's eyes looking back at me. What we discovered that night was, we did not need somewhere special to go for it to be special. We made it special. So I encourage you to change clothes and go. Go have your date and have your time together. Regardless of what you do, make it the best ever.

Conversation:
1. When was our last date?
2. When are we going?
3. What are we doing?

Prayer: Heavenly Father, in the name of Jesus, give my spouse and I time and money to date. Please allow us to find the importance of why we should continue in the courtship long after we are married. Allow the things that attracted us on day one to still attract us on day 2,001. Let us be made again anew in You. In Jesus name, Amen.

Budget...

Situations will come to remind you of where you are or where you are not. Do not allow them to. *The sufferings of this present time are not worthy to be compared to the glory that shall be revealed in us. Romans 8:18.* Some of the most trying times in your relationship will come when you are under financial distress. Do not allow these things to break you or interrupt the peaceful flow in your marriage. The Bible says in Ecclesiastes 10:19 *a feast is made for laughter, wine make life merry, but money answers all things.* However, it is imperative to educate yourself on what it will take for you and your spouse to get through the financial hardship and no matter what, do everything to protect your garden in the process.

How do you protect it? You have to be willing to sacrifice and save. Of course you want to have date nights, take your kids on trips, go shopping, and do all the things you did before. Totally understandable. However, we you cannot do all the things that you want, you have to become a bit creative, make those things happen, and find a way to entertain yourself. If possible, budget monthly for entertainment. Plan the date nights without dinner but desert. Find free events in your community that you can attend as a way to entertain your family. The key is not to spend money but to continue to spend time.

If you fail to plan, you plan to fail. When things get tough in your marriage whether that be finances, health problems, issues with the kids, family members, etc. you have a responsibility to iron out those wrinkles. Talk, talk, talk, and talk some more about the things you want to see and experience in your marriage. Most importantly, do not rush the process. You can find success in defeat and there is something very special about what you and your spouse will learn and who you will both become during the journey.

Conversation:
1. What is our current budget?
2. After monthly expenses do we have any extra?
3. What are some areas where we can save?

Prayer: Heavenly Father, in the name of Jesus, forgive us for bringing unnecessary drama and weight to our relationship because of our finances. We understand that you are Jehovah Jireh our provider so we will trust You to take care of all of our needs. No longer will we give time to unproductive conversations about the things we cannot change. We will no longer fuss, fight, and argue about money because we know where our help comes from. In Jesus name, Amen.

Laugh Out Loud...

Every other Wednesday was my day off and the strangest thing would always occur. I was never really off. Go figure. Wednesdays were almost always consumed with appointments and household chores. Of course they had to be done only to redo them all over again on Saturday night right after an intense pop warner football day with our son. Or there was always Sunday afternoon somewhere between church, watching the Chicago Bears and Carolina Panthers play, cooking Sunday dinner, prep work for the next work week, and finding time to watch one episode of Snapped. But this particular Wednesday was different. I decided to go with the flow and not worry if anything got done or not. I decided to live and laugh out loud with my husband all day.

We took our son to school and were off to breakfast. Before we sat down at the table I had already took a thousand selfies. He was a trooper though or maybe he is just use to it because after #18 if I didn't have one that worked; I was out of luck. We sat down, he ordered our breakfast and there we talked, ate, and laughed out loud. Everything apparently was funny that day or we just simply enjoyed each other's company. Either way, we laughed and laughed and laughed some more.

Afterwards we took a trip to the hospital to visit the sick but had to wait. While we waited, we laughed about everything and nothing at all. Still waiting 2 hours later and still laughing. Finally allowed to do what we came to do which was to pray. I still believe it is more gratifying for us than those who received prayer. I guess we talked, laughed, and prayed up an appetite because afterwards we found ourselves tucked away in a quaint, swanky pub downtown Charlotte, NC. There, we laughed and talked and laughed more and more. Couldn't tell you what it was about or why we laughed so much but we did.

Once our day came to a close I sat in the bed, gazed around the room, and noticed the laundry was not folded and put away. The bathroom was not as clean as much as I wanted and I still had ironing to complete. We did not follow our routine of cleaning. We really made no effort to go to the gym either. We simply enjoyed spending time together over breakfast, lunch, and dinner. Even in the shower we were joking and laughing.

I encourage you to take a break from the norm and just let your hair down with your spouse. Of course you cannot do this every day but take a break. Go to an amusement park or a place like Dave & Busters. Just the two of you. Go for a walk or just do something different. Do not plan it. Do something totally out of the norm and laugh out loud. It is the best medicine for the soul and if you can do that with the one you love, it will be a day well spent.

Conversation:
1. When is the last time we laughed out loud?
2. What do you remember it being like?
3. Do we have enough of this?

Prayer: Heavenly Father, in the name of Jesus, thank You for giving us laughter because we realize that laughter is good for the soul. Lord, we want to enjoy each other with the time you have given us to share. We are asking You to give us wisdom on how to marginalize our lives in order to have more time to live life more abundantly and laugh out loud. In Jesus name, Amen.

Iron sharpens iron...

In its simplest form ask your spouse these two rudimentary yet deepening questions.

a. What can we do more of?

b. What can we do less of?

If your husband or wife is a pleaser like my husband, they would probably say "we are great because we do this and this and this right and we are good baby and do not need any help." Uhmm hmmm. Sure you are. Close the book. You have made it. You get the "Couple of the Year" award. There is nothing else to work on and nothing else to make you better... Don't believe the hype. New love sometimes can be blind and very forgiving until it becomes dated. However, once you're settled in, you may get stuck with bad habits that are extremely difficult to break.

I would like to encourage you to challenge your spouse intellectually by making them tell you what the two of you can work on and what you need to let go of.

Examples of things to work on:

1. Sex. (of course my husband agrees that we should have more of it and less of Not having sex)
2. Being punctual.
3. Reading and praying consistently together.
4. Exercise.
5. Going to bed at a decent hour.

Examples of things to let go of:

1. Toxic friendships/relationships.
2. Excessive drinking and/or smoking. (anything that is detrimental to your health)
3. Opinions of others

These kinds of things could keep your relationship refreshed and enlightened. Work on a couple of these things for a period of time and watch your life transform. It will make you better.

Conversation:
1. What can we do more of?
2. What can we do less of?

Prayer: Heavenly Father, in the name of Jesus, thank you for the simple things in life. You said in your word that you would take the foolish things to confound the wise and today my spouse and I no longer want anything; any foolish, simple thing to be hidden from our sight. We believe by faith that our marriage will forever be healed, forever be free from confusion and forever be filled with love, trust, and honesty. We are going to listen for cues of problems that we have, be mature enough to handle them, and trust You to help us fix them. In Jesus name, Amen!

Growing apart?

This unfortunately happens more often than not in relationships. As you get older you and the love of your life may find yourself growing a part. What's interesting about those two words are the "growing" and "apart." Growing in your relationship is beautiful. Sometimes you do not need another date, although date nights are important. Sometimes you do not need another exotic vacation to rekindle the flame. Sometimes in order to get that old thing back or maybe something new and lively; you need to simply grow in some areas of your own life.

Education, promotion on your job, a different role in your church or serving in your community could very well give you the growth boost you need. Now, there is a flip side to that. If one of you are growing; it is imperative that both of you grow in your relationship. For example, if you decide to get your Master's degree, your spouse should do the same or its equivalent. Why? When you are furthering your education you are constantly learning. You're reading more, writing research papers, and having deeper conversations with other classmates and colleagues. You are being introduced to a whole new world and by default your desires, wants, and needs begin to change. Your appetite for growth enhances and that is just the beginning. You will begin to develop different interest and there is nothing wrong with that.

While you are busy working on you and making yourself better, your spouse should also be actively doing the same. If you can only afford and have time for one Master's degree, that is perfectly fine. Just make sure as one develop, each of you develop because when you do not, the commonality that you once shared will fade. Fading wants and desires doesn't suggest that the love is fading. It also doesn't prove that he is wrong and you are right. It is an indication that you are both evolving into something new and now that your interests are different; you have work to do. Good work. Work that brings new and fresh conversations. New and fresh fun. New and fresh relationship. New and fresh romance.

Conversation:

1. Do you have new interests?
2. How can we share in those together?
3. What one thing can we do together that will educate us, reward us, and bring us closer together? Examples: physical fitness class, bible course offered at the community college, financial class. etc.

Prayer: Heavenly Father in the name of Jesus, thank you for giving us access to earthly tools that will make us better. Our desire is to grow together versus apart. Please allow our accomplishments and successes to collectively bless and enrich our lives. We ask that those things will bring us closer than we have ever been before. We pray that those same things will bring You glory as You use us individually and collectively for your service. Allow us to now find opportunities of work, education, and/or physically training that will help us be a blessing to our spouse. Let these things be a blessing to us and not a curse, hindrance, or a stumbling block. As you individually graduate us into greatness, graduate the both of us into greatness. Make us both better for each other. In Jesus name, Amen.

Love is slow to anger...

After the third year of marriage my husband would jokingly call me snapping turtle. But what I have learned over the years is 90% of a joke is really the hidden, beautiful truth of what someone really wants to say to you, but doesn't have the courage to tell you. Only 10% is the actual joke. However, I was not unaware of why he called me snapping turtle because I knew that I was snapping at him. I was Ms. Snapper Snapping and although I loved him, out of frustration, I let him have it. I needed him to do more of whatever it was he was not doing and simply frustrated me. Initially, he found it amusing until the small stuff started to aggravate me to the point of annoyance. I would literally get upset to the point of anger all because he did not take out the trash. Sadly it happened more than once until my husband said, "babe, why are you so upset over nothing?" And he was right. I was upset over nothing and to be honest sometimes I didn't feel upset-it just became my natural reaction because I felt comfortable doing it. The one thing I will say is I wasn't trying to manipulate him because my husband is not going to do anything that he doesn't want to do. But I realized that I had a problem.

Psalm 103:8 The LORD is merciful and gracious, slow to anger, and plenteous in mercy.

In your relationship sometimes your cold, ugly, or distant reaction to a problem will only add more frustration to the situation. The important thing to do would be to sit down and discuss the reason(s) why you are vexed. It may not even be what you think it is. One day we sat down to discuss what my deal was but before I could say anything, my husband said that he already knew. He said it was probably years of pent up emotions of the times he did not help or do what I needed him to do. Now I have all the symptoms of an emotionally frustrated women and he was apologetic for it. He said that he was sorry that it took him so long to realize and understand what he was doing to me and sorry for pushing me into that position of anger and aggravation. He went on to say that his goal was to never put me into another situation that would cause me to snap at him. He said because it took time for me to get there, over time I became increasingly angry which meant it affected my mood about everything and probably not in a good way. The beauty is, he understood that if I was frustrated with him, at some point I was probably frustrated with every other thing or every other person I was in relationship with and he did not want to be the reason for anything negative coming from me. He valued my feelings, my life, and my heart carefully.

1 Corinthians 13:5 Love does not dishonor others, it is not self-seeking, it is not easily angered, it keeps no record of wrongs.

Your hindrance may not be something your spouse did or did not do. It could be an underlining problem or issue from your past that is surfacing into something totally unrelated. Find out what it is and tell your spouse about it. They maybe what you need to unlock the rage, pain, and hurt in your heart and be the balm needed to help you heal.

Conversation:

1. Is there anything that I have done or have not done that has caused you to be upset with me?
2. What can I do to make things better for you and for us?
3. I am sorry and I will do my best to never hurt you in this manner again.

Prayer: Heavenly Father, in the name of Jesus. I ask You for courage to admit when I have done wrong. I ask that You would give my spouse and I the heart of forgiveness and a short memory of the things that we have done wrong to each other. Allow us to love the way You love and never keep any records of wrong doings. Allow us to be willing to take ownership for our mistakes and love each other through it all. In Jesus name, Amen.

Use your words...

I remember when my son attended his first day of daycare. I, like most mommies was terrified. I did not want to leave him alone with complete strangers for eight hours daily because at one year old, he was learning to walk, talk, and his character was being formed. I personally did not want too much of anyone else's influence to form my son's opinions, character, or behavior. However, I also did not want my son to be so attached to me that he experienced separation anxiety. Thus, I decided to take him to daycare a couple of times a week in order to give him a happy medium.

While he was there I noticed that being around other kids was actually a blessing. He wanted to walk because they were walking. He tried different kinds of foods because they ate different kinds of foods and more importantly; he began to talk more than ever because they were talking. One of the tactics the caretakers would use when the kids wanted something was "use your words." It forced the children to attempt to speak words instead of using attentions getters such as acting out or misbehaving just to get what they wanted. Because it worked in school of course I implemented it at home. Over time my son became older, his communication skills became better and now he has no problems effectively communicating his wants and needs to his Dad and I.

Sometimes in our relationships, as elementary as it seems, we should use our words. It is not that we do not know how to speak clearly so our voices are heard but I do believe as adults, somewhere down the line we have lost our ability to effectively communicate. Or for some of us, we have never learned. If we did learn how to communicate, it was in some way distorted and difficult for anyone to understand. Yelling and screaming does not constitute as an effective way of communicating. Withdrawal is also a common tool individuals use to get their point across but has proven not to be a successful communication strategy. It is typically used as a form of manipulation to trick your spouse into giving you what you want. All of these will leave your conversations unfruitful and nothing will ever get resolved. If you are doing this, your spouse will become very resentful towards you and that is when division steps in.

I encourage you to use your words. In other words, do not make your spouse wreck their brain trying to figure out what is "wrong" with you. God did not call him/her to the prophetic so do not expect them to be a mind reader. You are hurting yourself and seriously damaging your relationship when you decide not to share your thoughts and feelings with your spouse. What tends to occur in these types of situations is their trust towards you dwindles and before long they just become immune to it. If you do see results it is only to pacify your childish behavior. It is a tactic they have learned to shut you up in order to go back to a calmer, inquisitive, and more loving conversation with someone else who has learned the importance of using their words...

Communication or the lack thereof is one of the leading causes of divorce in the country so, grow up. Use your words and challenge your spouse to take a different approach when they need to talk to you about what is on their minds. My advice would be, just talk.

Conversation:

1. What are some things that I do or how do I act when I don't use my words?
2. How does it make you feel?
3. How can I better communicate with you about the things on my heart?

Prayer: Heavenly Father in the name of Jesus, thank you for your infinite grace that covers us when we fall. Thank you for showing mercy towards us and giving us another opportunity to get it right. We ask that You would allow the Holy Spirit to guide us, order our steps, and help us communicate better. Don't allow us to harbor anger and resentment towards our spouse when we feel hurt. Give us courage to say how we feel nicely and maturity to be able to handle it. Help us to learn that we do not have to use hurtful words just to get attention from our spouse or to get them to do what we want them to do. Grant us patience so while you are working on us and making us better; we will be as patient with them as you have been with us when we error and with our flaws. Calm our fears and doubts about our inadequacies and allow us to trust your process. In Jesus name, Amen.

Just one of those Days... Don't take it Personal...

Today my husband wasn't sad, but melancholy I think. Either way he was not 100%. Instead of trying to figure out what was going on with him or worse, getting upset with him simply because he did not respond to me the way I thought he should; I let him have his feelings...

In relationships we have to understand that these feelings our spouse may have from time to time are not directed towards us. We are human and sometimes we act like it. Therefore, in these types of instances, do not try and force your spouse to talk about anything that is not really there. Let's face it; every day is not a glory, glory, hallelujah type of day although we want them to be. As long as you or your spouse are not swinging from one end of the pendulum to the next daily; occasionally being low on the mood elevator never hurt anyone. In fact, it forces you into a place of thought. What should happen is, you or your spouse, whoever is swinging should take this time to evaluate and see if there is something that is pulling them or you into a place of solitude. And let them figure it out. Typically the next day brings new mercies, new grace, and a new day for change. Until then, all they may need from you are kisses, hugs, love, or maybe space. Just don't bombard them with questions.

There is nothing wrong with you. There is nothing wrong with them. It's just one of those days...

Conversation:
1. Could I have done anything differently?
2. When I'm having a day what would you like me to do?

Prayer: Heavenly Father, in Jesus name, thank You for allowing me to feel the gamut of emotions from happy to sad, angry to joyous, and from hate to love. The constant change in my emotion reminds me of how much I need You and without You, I would fail. We pray that You would order our steps so that we are moving in the right direction together Lord. If we are having trouble in our day give us the right words to say to each other and let us have the right attitude towards each other regardless of what emotional state we may be in. I ask that You would touch our hearts so we might love and support each other in what we do and how we may feel. Thank You Jesus for Your love that is truly unwavering. We will take more of it in Jesus name, Amen.

I love you just the way you are…

I grew up in a home with my mother, grandmother, and my grandfather. We did not have much, but love was at the core of our family and that alone made us very rich. My grandfather was like my dad so when I dated, I looked for the same type of qualities in a man that I saw in my grandfather. He was tall, dark, and handsome. He was stoic but when you got to know him; he was a good hearted man and a very funny guy. Reminds me of my husband. In addition, he was a no nonsense type of guy as well. Thus, I was always taught there was a time and a place for everything. For the most part, I learned that if I wanted to be taken seriously; I had to put on my serious face, don't entertain silliness, and more importantly, don't embarrass myself. A bit harsh for a chap but that is not to say that we did not laugh or have fun because we did. However, most of everything else was a serious matter.

Until one gorgeous 70 degree day in Colorado Springs, Co, June of 2010 when I met Vincent "goofy boy" Weathers. My life went from smirks to smiles, from chuckles to outrageous laughter, and from stern looks to looks of merriment, cheer, and sheer glee. Don't get me wrong, I was a fun person to be around, but I sometimes struggled with letting loose. I would have to say, Vincent brought out the funny, sillier side of Shannon. He made me better.

Sometimes our spouses have something very special or unique about themselves that can be a true blessing to our lives. My husband taught me how to relax and live life a little without care of anything or anybody. Embrace the differences your spouse brings to the relationship. Don't let it aggravate you. Don't allow it to get on your nerves. Learn to love the quirky, unorthodox, weird things about your spouse. Those are the things that make your spouse special and make your relationship uniquely different; whatever that difference may be.

Love your spouse just the way they are…

Conversation:

1. Something that you do not know about me is that I like to....
2. Do I make you feel bad for being you?
3. How have I responded to you in the past?
4. What would you like to see or feel from me in the future?

Prayer: Heavenly Father in the name of Jesus, thank You for the opportunity to pray to You about our relationship concerns. We believe that You hear us when we call and because You love us, we will get results. We ask for your forgiveness today on the matters of not honoring who You have made our spouse to be. You have blessed them to be different, funny, smart, reserve, tall, short, handy, crafty, loving, thoughtful, caring, impartial, true, focused, spontaneous, and genuine. Because of their uniqueness I did not appreciate and some of their qualities I have taken for granted; I failed to value the joy it brings to our relationship. When I look at him/her, allow me to see what You see, understand the way You understand, and love how You love. Allow us to grow together in who we are in You and continue to fall in love over and over again with who we are in each other. In Jesus name, Amen.

Silence yourself and let him lead...

It got to a point in our relationship that I was done talking about what I needed from my husband. We both went to work for eight hours daily and both went to the gym. We both shared the responsibility of raising our son. Both had friendships to tend to. Both had bills to pay. Both were tired at night, but sometimes I guess I was more tired than he was because he always had energy for the "you know what." I guess he had a reserve tank of energy stored underground or something. I dunno. But the bottom line was we both had our own stuff to deal with. So, if our plates were both full, why didn't he help?...

I requested help with was household chores, regular maintenance on our cars, lawn services, and other miscellaneous jobs around the house. It is not that my husband could not or would not help, he would just get it done on his own time. That of course could have been when Jesus returned. In my heart I knew my husband was not trying to hurt me by not helping, but I was at the end of my rope with how long it took for him to get things done. I also came to the realization that the things that were important to me were not as important to him and regardless of how long it took him to finish, those things didn't matter to him. His concept was, as long as it was done, who cares how long it took him to complete it? Well I did and I grew very frustrated and exhausted trying to get him to understand. The fussing only got us nowhere fast, so one day I just made the decision, if it could wait, it did. I did not fold a handkerchief if he said he would. I let it stay on the couch, in the basket, or on the counter. It was extremely difficult at first but after a while, things started to get done. Trash was taken out. Clothes were stored and put away. He even started taking the initiative to cook more.

Watching him finally do the things that I asked him to help me with really blessed me. I felt like he was finally listening and that he cared. I did not take this time to remind him of how long it took to get his act together, nor did I decide to have the "it's about time" type of attitude. Instead, I decided to simply say, thank you. Before long, it was nothing for my husband to wash dishes, cook, and clean without me asking. It was a wonderful start and it came when I decided to take my hand and my mouth off the situation and let him lead.

As a woman, it is natural for us to get up; make breakfast, get ourselves ready, get the kids ready, and sometimes our husband too. In some cases, we lead and run the household. In my home, I set the tempo so when I am out of commission; my family has a hard time managing without me. They adjust, but it is not as comfortable as I make I, nor does it have my finesse. If we as women are not careful, that leadership role we possess will leak over into other areas where we should not lead. It can be very dangerous. Know your role and stay in your lane. Do not cause an accident in your marriage simply because you want to be in control of everything. Gracefully, serve in your calling as a wife, but allow your husband to be the head. Let him lead by serving you and your family his way; without your expertise, guidance, or advice.

Conversation:

1. What more can I do to help you with the things you need?
2. When I take initiative, how does it make you feel?
3. What plan can we put in place to help us lighten our load?

Prayer: Heavenly Father in the name of Jesus, thank You granting me with the patience I needed to endure this trial. Thank you for touching my spouse's heart with the love and support I wanted from him. Regardless of what we go through, allow us to continue to honor each other and do not allow us to take the other for granted. Let us cherish our spouse and fill all of their love tanks each and every day. In Jesus name, Amen.

Am I a victim or am I the culprit?

There should never be a time in your relationship when your determination to grow and evolve becomes intimidating to your spouse. In a previous relationship, I had the desire to go back to college and finish my degree. I just had my son who was coming up on one years of age and I had a sense of urgency to fulfill my dream of becoming an educator. My son's Godmother volunteered to babysit a few nights a week so I could go back to school. However, my son's father did not see it as a blessing. He argued me down about making sacrifices and used our son as a pawn to make me feel as if I were deserting him by leaving him with the sitter while I went to class. My argument to him was, he was also our son's parent and he should make as much of a sacrifice for him as I did. Besides, he was not in school and his job ended at 4:30pm. A few hours with the sitter weekly was not going to cause any harm to our son. This bickering back and forth only made matters worse and put a divide between us. The short of the story is, I did go back to school, against his will, and it made matters worse in our home. Now looking back I realize, he did not want me to go to school because he thought that it would make me more marketable for other men and potentially leave him. I left him anyway but not because of the degree. I left because he was very insecure and selfish. His own selfish acts lead us to divorce court.

Selfishness is a symptom of insecurity and if your spouse is upset with you because of your desire to improve, it is probably not about you. It is a deep rooted seed of insecurity that has manifested itself into competition, anger, and jealousy. Someone who is whole will always want to see you succeed. They will be your biggest cheerleader, your biggest fan, and will always encourage and exhort you and your achievements. Someone who is broken will make insults, tear you down, and give you one million reasons why you should not accomplish your goals. If you and your spouse are struggling in these areas, I highly encourage you to seek professional help. If your spouse is not interested, be patient with them, but begin to pray for him/her for God to remove whatever is causing the discord. Matters such as these only manifest into greater issues and serious problems that will be very damaging to your relationship. These complications do not get better on their own, so do not ignore them; it has to be dealt with.

Ephesians 4:2-3 Be completely humble and gentle, be patient, bearing with one another in love. Make every effort to keep unity of the Spirit through the bond of Peace.

Conversations:
1. Does my success intimidate you?
2. How can I say I'm sorry?
3. Do I encourage you enough?

Prayer: Heavenly Father in the name of Jesus, we lift our hearts and our voices to You in praise and we honor You for your goodness and your love. Father we understand, in order to keep the hate out of our hearts is to keep love on our lips. Our desire is to love each other the way Christ loves the church and in order to do that, we need your help. Please remove that which is malicious in our hearts and replace it with undeniable love. Search our hearts, find what has broken it, and fill it with love, compassion, joy, and peace because our desire is to be whole again. We want to please You and our spouse. We receive it now in Jesus name, Amen!

Trust

I remember when my husband and I first met and started
dating heavily. Not knowingly or deliberately, we fell fast
for each other and because of the spontaneity in our
relationship, all things opened up quickly. Our
conversation opened up and nothing was held back to
include good and bad relationship experiences, sex
partners, and insecurities that we had and may have still
been struggling with. We withheld nothing from each other
or at least that's what we thought.

One day during the dating year, after he'd already met my
son and things appeared to be perfect, I walked into the
living area where he was watching TV and said "I love
you." Then my boyfriend said "thank you." I had to
mishear him because the correct response was I love you
too, back at you, or something closer to I love you, but not
thank you. It's not like I gave him a glass of water after
spending a physically exhausting day out in the hot sun, or
I picked up his dry cleaning from the neighborhood
cleaners. I just expressed my love to him and the only
response was "thank you?" So, my reply was "I said, I love
you baby, did you not hear me?" And then what he said
next became a hard pill to swallow, but the best medicine
anyone could have ever given me.

He said "yes I know you love me and believe me, I love
you too, but I need you to trust me." And with that, he went
back to watching TV.

I was startled. His words pierced my heart as if someone
had plunge a knife into it. Suddenly, I realized even
through all the spontaneity, excitement, conversation, and
love that we seem to share, we were missing one vital piece
of the equation, trust. From there, I began to think about

how stagnant our relationship would be if I did not start trusting my soon to be husband. At that moment, I had to come to grips with the hard reality that my trust issues were not only real, they had nothing to do with him. It came before him and if he was willing to love me through it, I had an equal responsibility to get through it. Vincent deserved the best me and that meant all of me and not just the parts I wanted to share with him.

Are there some areas in your relationship that have kept you stagnant? Are there things that are weighing your relationship down? Could there be issues, past hurt, pain, and disappointment that you brought into your relationship knowingly or unknowingly that is causing your once spontaneous, fresh, romantic, and blossoming relationship to wilt and die? It is not too late. You can breathe life back into your relationship and get back what you once had back, or get what you never had. Tell yourself the truth about you and your situation, deal with it one issue at a time, and watch the spark return to your relationship.

1 John 4:18 there is no fear in love, but perfect love cast our fear. For fear has to do with punishment, and whoever fears has not be perfected in love.

The presence of fear is the lack of trust. You cannot adequately love your spouse if you do not trust them. What you are really communicating is that you do not completely trust God.

Conversation:
1. What poison(s) have I brought into our relationship?
2. My plans to fix it is?
3. I need you to support me this way...

Prayer: Heavenly Father, in the name of Jesus, thank You for bringing light to some dark areas of our lives and exposing it for what it is and what it has done to our relationship. We are excited that we no longer have to love in fear; for the presence of fear is unperfected love in us and your love is perfect. We will no longer live in fear of what might happen to our marriage because we now understand why we are not growing and what we need to do to fix it. We believe, faith without works is dead and we believe by faith the love we once shared and passion for each other has not run out. It has been suffocated under the issues that we are individually struggling with. Thank You for healing. Thank You for deliverance. Thank you Lord. Our lives will never be the same and with time, our relationship will be healed from all things. In Jesus name, Amen.

The Miscarriage…

There was a time in our relationship that my husband felt, we had it all together. That is not to say that he thought we were perfect, but he believed because everything went our way, everything would always go our way. I strongly advised him that life can and will happen to us regardless if we were in sin or not. We did not have to be bad for bad things to happen to us. I encouraged him to pray while things were good so we would have the strength to endure when things were not so good. Well, just as I expected, life happened…

We went through a season were everyone went before us. It appeared everyone else purchased homes, cars, and received promotions on their jobs before we did. More importantly, everyone around us was having babies- all except us and that was our prayer to God. A baby was what we wanted. We were not at all upset or angry about others being blessed. We were excited for them, honestly. I personally began praying with women who wanted to give up on having babies due to various reasons. I served as a support system for them and encouraged them to believe God no matter what. I strongly discouraged them to give up and quit and asked them to allow me to pray with them. For months, I begin to pray with these ladies and they would pray for me as well. After several months of praying, one of the ladies received a positive pregnancy test. Shortly thereafter, the other received her positive pregnancy test as well. God answered. I was thrilled. I knew that my turn was next. One month passed. No positive result. Two months passed. Again, no positive result. Then three, four, and five months passed, but nothing positive came in my direction. My attitude remained one of gratitude because I knew one day that God would honor my request. So my husband and I waited and while we waited, we learned how to be excited and praise God when others were blessed. Why were we not pregnant? I had no clue but I knew that if God blessed my neighbor, He was in the neighborhood.

I guess our time finally came because on Dec 10th, 2014 my husband and I learned that we were having a baby. We were elated. So very excited to finally be blessed with what we prayed for, a baby. The next day, we called the doctor's office to set up our first appointment and they asked us to come in the very next week. We came in, took another pregnancy test, and scheduled our first appointment to hear the heartbeat. It was a dream come true. We could hardly wait. We only told our family members and those closes to us and waited for January 2nd, 2015.

I will never forget that day… I could not understand how the best day and the worst day of my life could all be on the same day. We learned that there was no heartbeat and no baby. I had a miscarriage… The doctors were baffled and really couldn't give us an explanation. All I remember seeing on the ultrasound pictures through my teary vision was emptiness. Kind of what I felt at that moment. Empty. I turned my head. I couldn't bear looking at the scan. No sac was present. No small little pea. Nothing but scattered tissue. All I remember was looking into my husband's confused yet hopeful eyes as he urged the doctor to tell us something different but he did not. All he said was there was no baby. The ride home was long and the days that followed were unbearable. I just didn't understand why. I still don't.

After praying to my God, I asked why. Why would God give us a baby after all of the praying and fasting and believing just to take him or her away from us? I told God that I felt betrayed. I felt heartbroken. More importantly, I felt forsaken. Through my tears I begin to speak the word of God. *I was young and now I am old, yet I have never seen the righteous forsaken or their seed begging for bread. Psalm 37:25* As I spoke the word of God, God begin to speak His word back to me and He said. "I will never leave you or forsake you." This will work together for your good. At that moment, I knew the only way I would get through this, was through prayer. He then began to tell me that everyone has experienced a miscarriage. Male and female. He explained to me that a miscarriage is not limited to losing a baby. But the word miscarriage defined means an unsuccessful outcome of something planned. A miscarriage is simply failure, a breakdown, frustration, the undoing of something done, mismanagement, and nonfulfillment.

So my question to you is, what kind of miscarriage have you had? Are you still grieving over it? Have you allowed yourself time to mourn the loss and allowed God to heal you and fill you? As I write this, I am still mourning, but my heart is open to receive healing from my Savior.

For my last and final devotion, I would like to encourage married couples to hold on to each other while you are having a miscarriage. Sometimes no one else will be there for you and all you will have is each other. I remember that night after we left the hospital. In the wee hours of the morning, my husband and I wept, prayed, and held each other. All we had was each other. If your loved ones, family members, or friends are not there for you the way you would want them to be, excuse them. When you have a miscarriage and you are hurting, so are they. People are not trained on what to say nor do they totally understand what you are going through, so they may not know how to be there for you. Extend grace to them and however they are there for you, receive it in love. If you are angry, do not be angry with them or your spouse. Remember, they did not cause your miscarriage. Let them love you the way they express love. Because these times are delicate, you and your spouse have to be very sensitive to each other's feelings and be extremely patient with the other. Do not try and rush the healing process for your spouse. Recovery from a miscarriage takes time. So take your time. Only speak what you want to see into the atmosphere and if you cannot speak the word of God or anything positive, do not say anything until you can.

John 16:33 I have told you these things, so that in me you have peace. In this world you will have trouble. But take heart! I have overcome the world!

Conversation:

1. Our miscarriage was?
2. Are we still hurt by it?
3. How can we heal from it?

Prayer: Heavenly Father, in the name of Jesus we are hurting with the pain and grief of our miscarriage. We have lost our baby, our goal, and our dream. We do not know which way to turn from here so we are going to turn to You. We understand that You are always in control, even when it does not make sense and we do not understand. Our heart hurts, we are confused, we feel abandoned and we feel forsaken. But we know what we are not forsaken. We are loved. We are comforted. We are blessed. Our needs are met. We have the strength to face another day because of You. Our hope is in You. Our faith is in You. Our hope looks up to you. Our faith looks up to you. Through our tears, You never left us. Your love protects us. Today with all of the hope and faith that we have, we trust You. By faith, our hope, our joy, our peace, our love, and our faith are all restored. In Jesus name, Amen.

Now and For Always coming soon...